BUSINESS INTRODUCTION AND SUCCESS STRATEGY

Contents

BUSINESS INTRODUCTION.

A business introduction is a succinct description of a company or organization, including its goals, history, products, and services. A successful business strategy has a distinct vision, a well-thought-out plan for achieving that vision, and the flexibility to change as the market environment does. Important components of a winning strategy include:

Conducting extensive market research to comprehend market trends, rivals, and consumer needs.

Setting objectives and goals that are specific and measurable.

Developing a unique value proposition that sets the company apart from competitors.

Developing a thorough marketing strategy that successfully markets the business's goods or services.

Performance should be continuously monitored, analyzed, and adjusted as necessary.

Establishing and upholding trusting connections with partners, suppliers, and clients.

investing in the expansion and training of the business and its personnel.

MARKET BRIEF.

A paper or presentation called a "market brief" offers an overview of the most important data regarding a certain market or business. It often contains details on the market's size and development, significant participants and rivals, important trends and difficulties, and prospective investment or expansion prospects. Before making strategic choices, firms and investors often utilize market briefings to quickly grasp a market. In order to comprehend the dynamics of a certain market or sector, researchers, analysts, and policymakers may also utilize them.

SERVICE BRIEF.

A business service brief is a document that summarizes the important facts and details regarding a particular service that a firm provides. This might contain details about the function, target market, advantages, and cost of the service. The brief may also contain information on the characteristics of the service, any pertinent case studies or testimonials, and the company's contact information. It is often used as a sales or marketing strategy to assist prospective clients in appreciating the worth of the service and choosing whether or not to acquire it.

BUSINESS CARPORATE.

Corporate refers to the overall structure and organization of a business or company. A corporate status can refer to the legal status of a business, such as whether it is a corporation, partnership, or sole proprietorship. It can also refer to the financial and operational health of a company, such as its revenue, profits, and growth.

Product status refers to the current state or status of a specific product or product line offered by a company. This can include information such as the product's development stage, sales performance, and any updates or changes to the product.

CARPORATE INFORMATION.

A corporate business is a type of organization that is owned and operated by shareholders, who are represented by a board of directors. The board is responsible for making major decisions regarding the company's strategy and operations. Corporate businesses can take the form of corporations, limited liability companies, or other types of legal entities. They typically engage in activities such as manufacturing, retailing, or providing services. Corporate businesses are often publicly traded, meaning that shares of the company can be bought and sold on stock markets.

History.

Business history is the study of the development of businesses and the economic and social contexts in which they operate. It encompasses the history of various industries, such as manufacturing, retail, finance, and technology, as well as the history of specific companies and business leaders. The study of business history can provide insight into the evolution of economic systems, the impact of technology and innovation, and the role of businesses in shaping society. It also covers the history of management and business practices, labor relations, and the impact of government policies on businesses.

GOALS AND OBJECTIVES.

Business goals and objectives are targets that a company sets for itself to achieve over a certain period of time. These can include financial goals, such as increasing revenue or profits, or operational goals, such as improving efficiency or expanding into new markets. Objectives are specific, measurable, attainable, relevant, and time-bound (SMART) targets that support the overall goals of the organization. Setting clear and realistic goals and objectives helps companies to focus their efforts and resources, and measure their progress towards achieving their desired outcomes.

Staff growth plantings

A business staff growth plan is a strategy for increasing the size and capabilities of a company's workforce. This can include hiring new employees, training existing staff, and promoting from within. A staff growth plan can help a business to achieve its goals by ensuring that it has the necessary skills and resources to meet the demands of its customers and stay competitive in the marketplace.

There are several steps that can be taken to develop a staff growth plan. These include:

Assessing current workforce needs and skills gaps

Identifying areas where the company may need to expand or add new staff
Developing job descriptions and qualifications for new positions
Identifying potential sources of candidates, such as job fairs, recruitment agencies, and employee referrals
Implementing a training and development program to up skill existing staff
Establishing a performance management system to track progress and identify areas for improvement
Regularly review and update the staff growth plan to ensure that it remains aligned with the company's overall goals and objectives
A well-crafted staff growth plan can help a company to attract, retain and develop the best talent, and to be more flexible and responsive to changing market conditions and business needs.

LOCATION AND FACILITIES.

A business's physical location and the building or buildings that house it are referred to as its "location and facilities." The success of a business can be greatly influenced by its location, as some places may be more easily accessible to customers or have more foot traffic than others. The term "facilities" refers to the building or buildings that a company uses to conduct its operations. These buildings may house office space, warehouses, or manufacturing facilities. The standard and type of facilities can also affect how successfully a business operates.

MARKET AND COMPETITION.

A market refers to the group of consumers or organizations that are interested in a particular product or service. In a business context, a market can be segmented by factors such as geography, demographics, or purchasing behavior.

Competition refers to the presence of other businesses offering similar products or services to the same market. Businesses may compete on the basis of price, quality, innovation, or other factors. A high level of competition can drive innovation, improve service and lower prices for consumers. But excessive competition can lead to lower profit margins and a risk of bankruptcy for companies.

POSITION AND PHILOSOPHY.

A business service position is a job inside an organization that is in charge of offering a service to clients or other companies. Customer service agents, salesmen, and technical support professionals might all fall under this category. These jobs often include assisting consumers with their requirements and communicating with them.

A company's views and ideals about how it ought to conduct itself and engage with its stakeholders, including customers, workers, and other parties, are referred to as its "business philosophy." It provides the basis for a company's decision-making and may influence its culture and general course. A company philosophy may include a dedication to customer pleasure, an emphasis on innovation, or a conviction in morally upright and socially responsible behavior. A company's philosophy may play a significant role in differentiating it from competitors and drawing in clients, staff members, and investors.

MARKET AND GROWTH PROJECTION.

The industry or sector that a firm operates in, as well as the clients it services, are referred to as a business market. Market expansion is the term for a market's gradual growth in terms of both size and value. Market expansion predictions frequently take into account historical patterns, market research, and economic projections.

Changes in consumer behavior, developments in technology, and governmental regulations are all factors that might impact market growth. Market growth forecasts are used by businesses to guide their future planning and strategic decisions.

MARKET AND RESEARCH.

Market research is the process of gathering, analyzing, and interpreting data about a market, about a product or service that will be sold in that market, and about the past, present, and potential customers for the product or service. Research into the traits, spending patterns, location, and needs of your business's target market, the industry as a whole, and the specific competitors you face are all part of market research. Understanding the market context in which a firm operates and identifying and analyzing the needs of its clients and rivals are both beneficial. Businesses that perform market research can better understand their target market and come to wise judgments regarding their product development, marketing, and sales strategies. The various kinds of market research include primary research (such as

Defensive Strategy.

Management uses a defensive approach as a marketing tactic to protect their company from possible rivals. In other words, it's a battlefield where you must engage and defend your market share by maintaining the satisfaction of your clients and maintaining your profit.

To protect your company, you must be knowledgeable about the industry. Additionally, you ought to be aware of when to grow your company in the new market. Simply put, a defensive strategy involves leveraging your strengths and competitive advantages to outmaneuver the opposition. Methods for a Defensive Strategy
The management employs two defensive strategy philosophies, which are as follows:

ACTIVE METHOD.

The active strategy aims to thwart competitors who want to take your market share from you. Here, using an active strategy, you increase your product's marketing and promotion efforts while lowering your prices and offering discounts to drive away customers from your rivals.

PASSIVE METHOD.

Passive aims to prevent the competition from stealing your clients and market share. But the approach is somewhat lax. The actions you take when using the passive strategy are as follows:

Innovation in new products. Your attention is on creating and introducing the new product so that you can win back your customers.
Company growth. Your goal in this situation is to expand your business and organization into new markets. New customers would be drawn in by the market expansion.
Reconnect with Past Clients. To enhance sales, you get in touch with and retarget your previous clients. Methods for a Defensive Strategy
The management employs two defensive strategy philosophies, which are as follows:
When you firmly hold the top spot in your audience's thoughts, using this defensive tactic may be successful. If you have a positive reputation among customers in your industry and have developed a strong brand perception and brand loyalty, then protecting it to the hill is a wise strategy.
A challenger firm will have a tough task on their hands to change how consumers perceive your

company, organization, or product or service while you are the market leader, and an even tougher one to capture that mindshare for themselves.
If you decide to implement a position defense strategy, you are acknowledging the value of a positive brand impression and setting the stage to make sure that nothing compromises it. Around your brand, you are creating a fortress.

SERVICE DESCRIPTION.

The activities that support business but do not produce a tangible product are known as business services. For instance, one such business service that supports numerous other business services like shipping, procurement, and finance is information technology. Today, the majority of organizations lean toward these specialist business services.

When it comes to service provision, India is becoming very competitive and challenging other nations. Many foreign nations choose India as their preferred hosting partner for commercial services;

sometimes, they even choose to construct a branch office.

Learn more about the distinction between a businessman and an entrepreneur by clicking here.

Features of Business Services

The following lists business services according to their five criteria.

(1) Impermanence.

Since they are immaterial, you cannot touch them.

They lack their actual physical existence.

It can only be felt by the individual.

It is crucial to provide customers high-quality service so that they may have a positive experience.

Examples include instructors' instruction, patients' medical care, etc.

(2) Contradictory.

In contrast to actual things, services lack stability.

The service must be offered alone each time.

The demands and expectations of various clients vary.

Every time, the service provider must adjust the offering.

(3) Interdependence.

In the case of services, production and consumption occur simultaneously.
The goods can be produced today and sold later.

Inventory (4).

Services can't be archived for later use.
It has no tangible parts.
The service's supply and demand are extremely closely matched.
The consumer must get service as and when they want it.
The flavour of a Mc Donald's burger, for instance, cannot be preserved.
You may enjoy the voyage and store your airline ticket.

5. Engagement.

Services are offered in accordance with client needs.
Customers are involved in the process of providing services.
What Kinds of Services Are There?
These Are the Different Types of Services:

(1) **Commercial Services.**

Services utilized by commercial organizations in carrying out their business operations.
For instance, financial services, insurance, storage, and communications.

Social Services, Second.

These are given willingly to achieve societal objectives.
Giving workers and their families access to educational and medical facilities is one example.

3) **Individual Services.**

These are not inherently consistent.
Different customers need various services.
They are based on the priority of the client.

FOR INSTANCE, RESTAURANTS AND TOURISM.

Businesses that offer an activity or the completion of a task for a profit are referred to as service businesses. This job entails assisting a company or an individual in a variety of areas, including consulting, accountancy, transportation, cleaning, hospitality, travelling, and maintenance, among others.

These services are currently provided through both physical and virtual channels, such as web-based platforms and mobile apps. Customer service is a crucial component of an intangible activity that customers typically view as having value. On the other hand, compared to manufacturing or trade enterprises, these industries employ a greater proportion of people. They have a significant role in the majority of industrialized economies, and new technologies have made them more globally accessible.
From an economic standpoint, the tertiary industry or sector also refers to enterprises that provide services.

HOW IT WORKS.

Businesses are so much a part of daily life that it's tempting to take the business world for granted. Day after day, businesses give what we want fast, anciently, and with amazingly little hassle. Look around: practically every material good you're surrounded by right now was developed and given to you by some form of business.

What do apple cider and airlines have in common? Generalizations are challenging because businesses produce and deliver so many different things in so many different ways. As it turns out, quite a bit–if you know where to look. Here's how I define a business:

Every successful business: \creates or provides something of value that \soother people want or need \sat a price they're willing to pay, in a way that \satisfies the purchaser's needs and expectations and \provides the business sufficient revenue to make it worthwhile for the owners to continue operation

Take away any of these things–value creation, customer demand, interactions, value distribution, or port sufficiency–and you have something else than a business. Each aspect is both essential and universal.

As I analyzed each of those variables, I uncovered additional universal criteria. Understanding what people want is necessary for creating value.

First, you must grab their attention and interest in order to attract customers. People need to trust you to deliver on your promises before you can close a sale.

Reliable exceeding the customer's expectations is necessary for achieving customer satisfaction. It is necessary to generate more revenue (finance) than is expended in order to sustain profit.

No matter who you are or what industry you work in, none of these tasks are particularly complex, but they are always required. Your company will prosper if you execute them well. If you perform them ineffectively, your company won't last long.

Two additional components, people and systems, are fundamental to every business. Every company was founded by individuals and relies on the support of their customers to continue operating.

You need to have a solid understanding of how people typically think and act in order to understand how businesses operate. This includes how people make decisions, carry those decisions out, and interact with one another.

Recent developments in psychology and neuroscience are shedding light on why people act in certain ways and how we can change our own behavior to interact with others more successfully.

Contrarily, systems are the unnoticed frameworks that bind every organization together. Every company, at its core, is made up of a set of repeatable procedures that lead to specific outcomes.

No matter if you're working with an automotive assembly line or a marketing campaign, it's possible to find ways to enhance current systems by understanding the fundamentals of how complex systems function.

I tested the concepts in this book's principles with my clients and readers for several years before I wrote it. They were able to start new businesses, get promoted, and go through the entire product development process (from idea to first sale) in several instances in less than four weeks by comprehending and putting these "business mental models" to use. They also received job offers from prestigious corporations in the corporate and academic worlds.

Since they are useful, these ideas are crucial. You'll find it noticeably simpler to accomplish what you set out to do—and you'll have more fun along the way. You'll be able to add more value for others and improve your own financial situation.

Nearly many of these problems do not stem from inadequate management of affairs. It's not even that the incorrect things are being done. True, the right things are usually done—but ineffectively. What explains this seeming paradox? The foundational presumptions upon which the organization was established and is now operated are no longer valid. These are the underlying presumptions that guide an organization's conduct, guide its choices of what to do and what to avoid, and specify what the organization means by meaningful outcomes. These market-related presumptions are made. They focus on identifying consumers and rivals, as well as their values and behavior. They discuss a company's strengths and disadvantages as well as the dynamics of technology. These presumptions pertain to how a business is compensated. They are what I refer to as a company's business philosophy.

Every organization, whether it is a company or not, has a philosophy of the business. A sound theory that is focused, coherent, and unambiguous is, in fact, very effective. For instance, German politician and philosopher Wilhelm von Humboldt created the Institution of Berlin in 1809 based on a completely novel philosophy of the university. And for more than a century, up to the emergence of Hitler, his philosophy governed German academic life, particularly in terms of scholarship and scientific investigation. Georg Siemens, the founder and first CEO of Deutsche Bank, the first universal bank, had a crystal-clear vision for the company in 1870: to utilize entrepreneurial financing to reunite a still-rural and fragmented Germany via industrial growth. In spite of two world wars, inflation, and Hitler, Deutsche Bank has maintained its position as Europe's top financial institution for 20 years after its foundation. And in the 1870s, Mitsubishi was established based on a distinct and entirely novel

conception of business, which allowed it to become the leader in a young Japan within 10 years and one of the first really global companies within another 20.
Similar to this, the theory of business explains both the difficulties experienced by corporations like General Motors and IBM, which have dominated the American economy throughout the second part of the twentieth century, as well as their success. The reality that their conception of the company no longer holds true is what really underlying the present ailment of so many significant and prosperous firms throughout the globe.

SAMPLE CUSTMOR.

A sample customer is a representative group of people or businesses that a company engages with or has done business with in the past as a member of its target market. In order to obtain information and insights on the tastes, habits, and demands of a particular target market, sample customers are employed in market research. This aids companies in determining the best product development, marketing, and sales tactics and improving their understanding of their target market.

Businesses might choose to sample their clients using a variety of techniques, including stratified sampling or random sampling. When doing research, a company will choose a random sample of consumers from its target market. When a company splits its target market into distinct groups, or strata, and then chooses a sample of consumers from each stratum, this is known as stratified sampling. The sample is more likely to be representative of the total target market using this strategy.

It is crucial to remember that both the sample size and the sample should be representative of the population of interest. The sample size has to be sufficient to be statistically significant. If not, the research's findings could not be accurate or dependable.

REQIREMENTS.

Business requirements are a collection of guidelines that specify what an organization requires in order to operate efficiently. These needs may include infrastructure, employees, procedures, and technology. They may be used to assess the efficacy of current systems, goods, or services as well as to direct the creation of new ones. In order to create, develop, and deploy solutions that meet the aims and objectives of the company, business requirements are often acquired via a process of stakeholder involvement and analysis The target audience is taken into consideration while defining the needs and requirements for a project. It explains the motivations for developing a certain project, who will use it, what advantages users will experience, and how the project's success will be measured. The project's creation process is not specified in the business requirements.

An analyst must first identify the important stakeholders, which will always include the company owners or project sponsors, before compiling the business requirements. They often include involve the end user/customer and subject matter experts. BABOK 2.0 lists regulators (who could impose new regulatory requirements as a consequence of the project) and implementation subject matter experts as additional stakeholders from whom an analyst may elicit needs (who may be aware of capabilities currently present in or easily added to existing systems). To fully complete a deep discovery of business needs, these stakeholders must be extensively screened and questioned. The project's current documentation must also be carefully examined.

Purchasing movie tickets will serve as an example project to further illustrate what business needs look like. Consider a chain of 400 cinemas that saw a drop in ticket sales. Numerous consumers were polled, and the results revealed that people were choosing less inconvenient forms of amusement instead of waiting in line at their ticket booths. Customers said they would prefer to rent a movie or sign up for a movie rental service rather to deal with the aggravation of standing in line for ten minutes. The chain's business analyst suggests a method to enable consumers purchase their tickets online and print them in advance, saving time for customers and money for the firm, after considerable discovery with a restricted group of colleagues.

SERVICE MANAGEMENT.

An analyst must first identify the important stakeholders, which will always include the company owners or project sponsors, before compiling the A framework or method for managing and improving company services is known as business service management (BSM). It entails using ITSM best practices and technologies to enhance the provision and functionality of business services. BSM often comprises the administration of service-level agreements (SLAs), other performance indicators, and monitoring of business-critical services and applications. BSM aims to increase the overall efficiency and effectiveness of IT operations by aligning IT services with the demands and objectives of the company..

FACILITIES AND CAPTIAL EQIPMENT.

The location and infrastructure that a company uses to conduct its operations are referred to as business facilities. This may include any structures that are required for the operation of the company, including as buildings, warehouses, retail locations, and so on. A business's machinery, trucks, and other huge, pricey pieces of equipment, among others, are referred to as capital equipment. Because they are utilized to produce income over a long period of time, these goods are regarded as capital.

Making it possible to achieve the rising standards of living that people have a right to expect is business's main challenge. The fundamental technique for achieving this goal will continue to be mass production, but we need to increase capital investment quickly to achieve higher productivity at lower unit costs. Spending a lot of money on research encourages capital investment

and will lead to the replacement of a lot of old gear. New and better goods created by technology advancement will force change.
The idea that a capital investment programmed primarily entails replacing outdated gear has undergone a clear change. When thinking about capital investments, we are no longer mainly concerned with the physical life lifetime of equipment. The best possible economic life cycle of an equipment or plant must now be taken into account. We choose contemporary tools and gear that can provide a product of greater quality at a reduced cost and with less waste.
Long-term goals, upcoming technological advancements, the need for new goods, and other aspects unique to each organization must all be taken into account when making capital investment choices. These factors must show the impact on stock dilution, lower profits from substantial early-year amortization, and the amount of time it will take for earnings to justify the additional facilities.

Physical items purchased for a productive activity are known as capital equipment. These products are frequently purchased by businesses in order to grow their operations or to keep up with new methodologies or technological developments. They are typically recorded as fixed assets from an accounting standpoint, but per U.S. accounting regulations, they must be valued at more than $5,000 and have a longer than one-year expected life span in order to qualify as such. When it comes to capital equipment spending, some industries spend significantly more than others.

The operation of aircraft (equipment) accounts for the majority of an airline's revenue, making it a capital-intensive industry that frequently invests more in equipment than other sectors. Conversely, manufacturing companies require more capital than service companies do. These things include, among others, machinery, trucks, lifting systems, inventory transportation equipment, and warehouse racks.

CLIENT SERVICES.

The numerous ways a business assists its clients or customers are referred to as business client services. This might include things like account administration, technical support, and customer service, among other things. Business client services aim to make sure that clients are happy with the goods or services they have bought and that any problems or complaints they may have are resolved as soon as possible. While some businesses may have specialized client service teams or departments, others may combine various internal teams with outside partners to provide client services. There's an overarching trend in the client service business. In fact, a week doesn't go by in which we don't have a similar conversation with a company in the throes of the agency search process. They need more brand awareness, their competitors are dominating the press, and their board wants to know what the plan is to change that. They've heard that SHIFT can solve the problem and they want to know what we'd do.

Us: "Why do you think you're not currently getting the type of coverage you need and want?"

Prospect: "I have no idea. We have good spokespeople, our experts have bold opinions, and we're doing something different in the market. But, time and time again, we see articles we sh In order to provide excellent client services, it is crucial to have a thorough awareness of your clients' demands. Understanding their expectations of your business will make it easier for you to meet those expectations and provide them with the goods and services that best meet their requirements. Understanding the demands of your customers also entails paying close attention to their preferences. You may give exceptional customer services by paying close attention to factors like communication preferences, response times, and product and service kinds.

FAIR TRADE.

It's crucial to make sure you engage in ethical selling if you want to keep your customer connections based on mutual respect and trust. In order to generate a profit, ethical selling involves refraining from overcharging or providing consumers services and items they don't genuinely require. By doing this, you risk damaging your client connections and jeopardizing their faith in your collaboration.

Make sure to leverage your in-depth knowledge of their wants to offer them items and services that are truly valuable to them as well as answers to their difficulties. In the end, your clients could be appreciative of your sincere service, leading to higher client satisfaction, a favorable corporate reputation, and a rise in client retention.

RESPONSE TIME TO CLIENT ISSUES.

A timely reaction to the inquiries and worries of your clients is an additional critical component of good client services. Make sure to give your customers the information and tools they require

to rapidly get answers to their inquiries so that they know they are respected and recognized by your company. A thorough help desk or a simple service ticket system is two examples of this.
The importance of thorough replies may be equal to that of rapid ones. You should pay close attention to your client's worries and demonstrate your understanding of their viewpoints. If you want to accomplish this when speaking with a customer, think about using active listening techniques like paraphrasing and asking clarifying questions. You can develop solutions that fully address their challenges by having a thorough awareness of their worries.ould have

QUALITY CONTROLS.

In business, quality control is the process of ensuring that products or services meet a predetermined level of quality before being made accessible to customers. This may include testing, inspections, and other methods of determining the caliber of a commodity or service. Quality control is essential to ensuring customer happiness and to aid in preventing defects or issues that might lead to consumer complaints or returns. Quality control may also benefit a business's brand reputation and customer loyalty.

SOLES AND PROMOTIONS.

Sales made to other companies or organizations are referred to as business transactions. A sales force, online platforms, in-person meetings, or other methods may all be used to make these sales.

Promotions are marketing initiatives used to raise brand recognition and boost sales of a product or service. Advertising, special offers, competitions, and other rewards can all be included in promotions. Businesses may use promotions to increase sales, draw in new clients, or move inventory. Request evaluations from your consumers after making their purchases and your items shareable. Before making a purchase, 91% of shoppers read at least one review. Because the customer has no motivation to oversell, reviews increase the credibility of your company. Although negative evaluations may seem harmful at first, they really serve you well in the long term.

By 67%, negative reviews may increase conversion. Customers believe that companies with both good and negative evaluations are more honest. However, three unfavorable evaluations may persuade 67% of customers to remove items from their shopping cart. Strike a balance between fixing the areas you've been asked to work on and reacting to the unfavorable feedback. This increases the likelihood that 88% of consumers will ignore the unfavorable feedback. In the corporate environment, promotions are essential to employee recruitment and retention. Personnel are likely to stop interacting with a company for a lengthy period of time without the right usage of coaching and incentives. Competitors lure top personnel away from other businesses by providing workers with better compensation and perks. Promotions provide employees these types of incentives so they won't feel compelled to quit their employment.

Employees are motivated to perform more and try harder to please their supervisors since there are promotion channels available in the workplace. This is the underlying principle of worker retention and incentive programmes. It also motivates workers to put in more effort and achieve higher standards of excellence so they may contribute more to the company. Businesses raise their performance standards for all employees by issuing promotions, giving them an incentive to perform well and pursue new chances.

BUSINEESS DIRECT SALES PROCESS

Selling products or services to other companies or organizations is referred to as business sales. These sales may be made through a number of methods, including in-person interactions, internet platforms, and sales teams.
Marketing initiatives to raise a product or service's visibility and sales are referred to as promotions. Advertising, discounts, competitions, and other rewards are all examples of promotions. Promotions may be used by businesses to improve sales, draw in new clients, or move inventory.

discussing the direct sales process in business
A technique for selling products or services directly to customers through in-person interactions, usually one-on-one, is called direct sales. The terms "person-to-person" and "door-to-door" sales are also used to describe this method of selling.
There are typically several steps in the direct sales process: Prospecting is the process of locating potential clients and compiling a list of leads.
Contacting the prospect: Making initial contact with the potential customer, usually through a phone call or in-person meeting. Qualifying the prospect: figuring out if the potential customer is a good fit for the product or service being offered and if they are financially capable of doing so. Introducing the product or service to the prospect:

Outlining its features and advantages for them. Addressing any reservations or queries the potential customer may have regarding the good or service. Getting the prospect's approval to purchase something is known as closing the sale.
Maintaining contact with the customer after the sale to check on their satisfaction and look for chances to make more sales.
For businesses looking to expand their customer base and increase revenue, direct sales can be a useful strategy. It may, however, be a time-consuming and expensive operation. Your initial impression of direct sales may be of a well-meaning buddy pitching health pills and powders for a multi-level marketing business.

Although technically direct selling, it illustration doesn't do the direct sales paradigm justice. Direct sales have taken place if you stood in line for the new phone in front of the Apple Store. 41.6 million clients made purchases via direct sales channels in 2020 alone, while the number of businesses employing direct sales increased by almost 14 percent.

Because of this, direct sales sometimes have a poor name, yet when done well, it may be one of the most profitable sales options for a business.

We'll go through the details of direct sales in this article and explain how it can help you, your clients, and your bottom line.

ITERNAL SALES FORCE.

An internal sales force is a group of staff members tasked with promoting a company's goods or services to other divisions or departments within the same organization. This is distinct from an external sales team, which is in charge of marketing to clients outside the business. An internal sales force might be helpful for a business with many divisions or for a business looking to expand cross-selling prospects with its current clientele. A Guide to Internal Communication for Small Businesses Team communication is expected by workers as a crucial organizational component, not only s politeness. According to a recent research, there are several ways in which what managers and workers anticipate from communication varies. Only 39% of American workers believe that their company responded to changes linked to COVID-19 in a straightforward manner. In addition, 48% of workers think their company did a good job of informing them about the epidemic.

The findings are unmistakable: there is disagreement between employers and workers on the most effective form of communication. When these realities are combined with the growing calls for radical corporate openness, small company owners are faced with a completely new communication environment. Here's how you create a simplified communication plan for properly distributing vital information, whether it's a one-time announcement or a daily all-hands meeting.

LISENCING.

Obtaining legal authorization to run a company in a particular jurisdiction is done via the process of business licensing. This usually entails acquiring a license from the government or a regulatory authority, which authorizes the performance of certain kinds of commercial operations inside the territory. Various businesses and activities, including retail sales, manufacturing, professional services, and more, may need business licenses. Depending on the sort of company and the jurisdiction, several steps may be required to get a business license, although in most cases an application, supporting materials, and payment are required. Additionally, as a condition of keeping their license, firms may be subject to continuing compliance and reporting obligations.

www.ingramcontent.com/pod-product-compliance
Lightning Source LLC
LaVergne TN
LVHW020532160826
845677LV00015B/4007

* 9 7 9 8 3 7 5 2 7 0 3 2 6 *